Things People Do:

WHEN THEY FIRST JOIN THE MILITARY

Starring Brofus Collinbean
& Lonely Mcknightus!

Stupid things people do when they first join the military©2010 by Donte Sams.
All rights reserved. No part of this book may be reproduced or transmitted in any form or by any means, electronic or mechanical, including photocopying, recording or by any information storage and retrieval system, without written permission from the author, except for the inclusion of brief quotations in a review.
Published by: Vision publishing, Newport News, VA

ISBN-13: 978-1-4507-1163-0

Editing by: Beth Bruno
Published in the United States of America

Dedication

I want to dedicate my book first to God all mighty, nothing is impossible with God, my dad Thomas Sams(Big Sam) my source of wisdom, knowledge, understanding, and my back bone, my mom Jackie Sams (B.J) my love, comfort, inspiration, the center of my drive, my best friends, Charles (Hov) and Tori (T.T) Williams, my support, Aden and Avery, Andre Mayo, Uncle Reggie_(Big Will), Kelvin_(one friend comes closer than a brother), Andre Mayo, Marylyn, James and Mclean, Baron Jones, Uncle Eric, Uncle Neil, Joshua, and Marlene. Aunt Dee Dee, Charlene Hope, Maurice Pinkston, Ned (skate this), Mr & Mrs. Tracey, Al Lee and Amanda Lee, Al lee Jr. and Alexis Lee, Morris Doyle (Jodi). Gena Moore, Monica, I love you R.I.P, Capt. Robbins of (S.O.I west 2006), Capt. Madeins_ (C.O H&S company 2006), First Sgt. Winfree, Sgt.Maj. Cook, SSgt. Petithomme, Sgt. Mayers, GySgt. Taylor, SSgt. Ramierez, GySgt. Hull, First Sgt. Flower, SSgt. and GySgt. Mayhue, GySgt. Johnson, the Marines of Norfolk N.O.B, SSgt. G (R.I.P). The Marines from Rota, Spain who wanted to see my down- fall_ (what you meant for evil God meant for good, I love you all), Sgt Major. Simms, Darius, Darrnell and little D Prigmore, Monica Greene, Kelley Granger, Brandon Dudley aka Mr. Dudley, Wayne, Ernie Built, Pastor Glenn and his wife for the spiritual teachings at Bethel Temple Hampton, Bad news and the other cities in the 757, Heritage High school grads of '03 & '04, Newport News, VA, single mothers, single fathers, military wives, my troops overseas doing what they have to do for this country, the POW's, wounded in combat, the ones who came before and lost their lives for our country.

CONTENTS

1. BUY BRAND NEW CARS
2. GET CREDIT CARDS
3. BUY THINGS FROM E-1 & UP STORES
4. DRINK UNDERAGE
5. YOU ARE NOT A CIVILIAN ANYMORE
6. MARRY THE FIRST PERSON THEY HAVE SEX WITH
7. MARRY IN THEIR FIRST 4 YEARS
8. SPEND MOST OF THEIR MONEY ON ALCOHOL
9. DRINK THEIR ENLISTMENT AWAY
10. BELIEVE THEIR RECRUITER
11. THINK THEY HAVE AN OPINION
12. MARRY A WOMAN WHO KNOWS MORE ABOUT THE MILITARY THAN THEM
13. GO A.W.O.L. OR U.A
14. FOLLOW THE WRONG CROWDS
15. GO HOME ON LEAVE AND LIE
16. DO DRUGS
17. GET CONTRACT MARRIAGES
18. GET D.U.I'S
19. DON'T USE CONTRACEPTIVES
20. DON'T SAVE MONEY
21. PUT THEIR S.G.L.I IN THEIR GIRLFRIENDS OR BOYFRIENDS NAME

Starring Brofus Collinbean

1. Buy Brand New Cars

Problem:

There is nothing wrong with buying a new car my enlist men. But when is the right TIME? Not when you first join, that is for sure. You sign up as an E-1 or E-3. The E-1, as of 2010, makes $1447 a month, and an E-3 makes $1706. Some people might think that is a lot of money. However, but that's before you buy a new car without a credit history. If you notice, there are many car dealer ships near military bases. This is for a reason. Their signs will say, "Good credit bad credit, no credit E-1 and up." E-1 and up meaning, they know that you are going to get paid on the 1st and 15th. The military pay chart is easy to find; just "Wiki it". And don't forget your rank is on your ID. When you walk on to a dealership lot those dealers can tell you are the "F.N.G" (Freaking New Guy), the "BOOT", so they feed off of it. They prey on you. They are going to show you a car that they obtained from an auction, or a brand new one and sell it to you at the maximum price. If you don't have enough, that's cool because Pioneer Services will give you all the money you need at the highest interest rate allowed by law. Pioneer Services are "Military loans from $500-$10,000", which "You can repay your debt in manageable payments with flexible terms up to 36 months". But remember this... the car that you want to buy has a high interest rate as well. Many people at the age of 18-20 have not established credit, which is almost like having bad credit. So what do you do? You sign paper work for the car because you like it and it makes you feel good. As an enlist man who makes $1447 a month. Oops, I forgot about taxes. Just because you serve, doesn't mean that you don't pay taxes. Now we are at about $800, and that is me being nice. Your new car payment will probably be $400 a month, from a back alley financial institution at 18% because Navy Federal will not give you the loan, due to your nonexistent credit history. That would leave your total at $400. Oops, I forgot about insurance. You are under 25 and single, so that will be about $200 a month for full coverage because when you buy your $20,000, car don't think that you are not going to have full coverage. The bank will laugh at you. Check your stats, you are down to $200 bucks. You know something? I'm slow. I forgot about gas. That new Chevy Tahoe is sexy and the Chevy Camaro too, and you like to drive, so the gas will cost you $100, and once again I'm being nice, we both know it is more. You have $100 bucks left, if that. If you are stationed somewhere like California, go ahead and chalk it up because your money is gone. However, you have a very nice car.

Solution:

What most military members don't know is that after 6 months you can refinance with a good credit union like Navy Federal Credit Union and get a lower interest rate. Here is the kicker: the $400 payment you were making for 6 months or more to that back alley financial intuition was all going for interest, not for the principal, so it was not paying down the cost of the car. The check you get to refinance will be for the amount that you bought the car for 6 months to a year ago. "One team one fight." You have joined the United States Armed Forces where there is a lot of good mentorship, meaning people who have been in past one enlistment and are now senior in rank. Don't ask the person you joined with for advice. They might leave the car lot with the same deal you got, and if you decide to buy the car anyway make a decision based on research and not emotions. Do your research, ask questions, call your insurance company get a quote, READ and UNDERSTAND the contract, let me say this again READ AND UNDERSTAND THE CONTRACT. Here is a thought Go out and grab a nice 6 or 7 thousand dollar car that has low payments and reliability. That way you have more money in your pocket. For those who have that "I can do it by myself" or "I know what I'm doing" mentality, you can, but don't ever think you can't call mom and dad and ASK! Your parents or guardian love you and want the best for you. You can count on parents to be honest. They might yell, say you are dumb, but they are acting like that out of love and they don't want you to make the same mistakes they made. Parents, I know you love your grown ass babies, but if they don't listen it is ok. They are in the learning phase in which they will learn from their mistakes and grow. If they fail, don't say, "I told you so." Concentrate on the solution, not the problem.

2. Get Credit Cards

Problem:

You hear it all the time when dealing with credit cards; if you have not here is a first. Whatever you spend you are going to have to pay back and some, credit cards are not free money. Credit Cards can be good or bad--good if you have discipline and bad if you don't. If you use a credit card and pay off the balance every month it will help you establish a good credit rating. Don't go to the mall and shop, and then go to the club and pop bottles with the credit card; yes, clubs do take credit cards. When you get the bill in the mail you will see the minimum payment in a little square box and it reads $30 even if the balance is $5,000. Then you say to yourself, "It nothing but a G thang baby! All you want is $30? Take it"! The credit card company is saying, "Ain't nothing in this world a free thang baby. Here is 24% interest; take it!" I can go on and on about credit cards; there are many books that can teach you how to avoid getting burned.

Solution:

READ READ READ READ! Once you are done reading, read again. If you decide to get a credit card try and pay off the balance before the interest occurs. Read and understand what you are signing. If you decide to get out of the military make sure it is with good credit, some money in your pocket and debut free. If you spend like crazy without a credit card, imagine yourself with one. Don't go out and get a credit card. There are many books that can help you understand what you are getting into if you decide to sign up to get a credit card. The most neglected tool to help make you more successful is reading.

3. Buy Things From E-1 & UP Stores

Problem:

What I'm talking about is not a Best Buy or a Fry's. I'm talking about USA Discounters. They love the military. I had forgotten the name, so I "Googled" USA Discounters and bam!, I found "Military and Civil service approved." I know you want a laptop or a big screen T.V. to go in your barracks room and that is fine. If you are paying 24% interest on your 40-inch TV, is it really worth it? I know that you are like, "Hell yeah." Flip the page because you are not thinking straight.

Solution:

Do I have to say it again? READ READ READ! Don't make impulse purchases. Do your research and if you don't understand ask your leadership. Pick up the phone, call home and ask your mom and dad. Don't ask your friends that are your age, because that is where they got their T.V. They too are still learning how the world works. Take your time, save some money and get what you want without an interest rate or a payment because you bought it out-right. What I mean is: Don't save $1500 and buy a $1500 TV; buy a $1000 TV and save $500. That way you have some extra change in the bank. I know that it is easier said than done and, yes, it takes discipline to make that happen.

4. Drink Underage

Problem:

If you are going in the armed forces or you just joined, you are going to hear this a lot. If you are underage don't drink because you can get into a lot of trouble, loss of rank, restriction, extra work, or more duty. Those things can and will happen. I think that it really depends on your leadership, (if you don't know what I mean by that statement you will see once you are in). Let me give you an example. If you are liked, do what you are told, come to work on time, and you are at the top of your game against your peers. Then if you are spotted underage drinking they might look away. However don't put yourself in a situation where your shop, section or leadership absolutely can't help you.

Solution:

With the statement I mentioned earlier comes another statement. If you defend your country why can't you have a drink? I understand this statement completely. I'm not going to tell you not to drink if you are underage, because you are grown men and women; however be careful how you do it. Don't hang out in the smoke pit; don't go to other people's rooms with a lot of military members around; don't go out in town or walk around the base drunk. That is what I mean by putting yourself in a situation where your shop or section can't help you. Drink in your room with the door closed, chill and relax. Here is another approach; get stationed overseas where the legal drinking age is 18; then you can drink as much as you like responsibly. When I was in Spain, Marines were drinking it up. If you drink, control yourself. Being drunk is not an excuse to not be in control. You must control your alcohol intake, don't let it control you.

5. You're Not A Civilian Anymore

Problem:

This might be a shock but "YOU ARE NOT A CIVILIAN ANYMORE, TIMMY"! You are wondering what I mean. I mean it is time for a "CHANGE." You are now in a structured, disciplined environment. You don't understand what I mean. What I mean is: Stop dressing like thugs! Stop doing drugs! Nobody is going to wake you up so you can make it to work on time. Your Mama is not going to be there to wake you up. You always have to maintain a clean military appearance, even when you are not in uniform.

Solution:

Change can be good as long it makes you better. Switching from light liquor to dark liquor is not the change I'm talking about. Do things differently. Dress more professionally and have a clean appearance. When you put on your civvies people will respond to you differently. Don't go home on leave and sell drugs like you did before. Don't even hang out with people who do. When you go home on leave you will see the same people doing the same thing. You have decided for whatever reason to join the military. I think people join because they are seeking change, a better life or that is the only way the judge won't throw you in jail. Put it like this: You are coming from an unstructured environment where you could basically do whatever you wanted to a certain extent, to a disciplined structured environment where your surroundings are constantly changing. Those who don't adapt to the military lifestyle adapt to their early discharge or separation papers. You have joined, or have considered joining the Armed Forces, knowing that there is going to be a lifestyle change. So let the military put something in you and you take something from it. Don't swim against the current; swim with it, I promise that you will like the results better.

6. Marry The Person They Have Sex With

Problem:

I want you to understand something… just because she or he gives you some booty doesn't mean they love you. I have seen many enlist men get stationed somewhere away from home, meet a guy or girl, have sex and think they are in love. You are not in love; you are in lust. Don't think for a moment that he or she loves you. Let me tell you who he is, I call him "Lonely Mcknightus" the spirit of loneliness. You are far away from home, no family is around, you are missing home, and all of your friends from back home. The feeling of love and comfort leaves then loneliness kicks in and Lonely Mcknightus comes by to chill with you. At that point somebody offers you an invite to a club and you go because you are lonely and you agree because the Lonely Mcknightus is around; you can't see him but you can feel him. You go to the club and meet someone that you think is very attractive (think about that). You get their number and call. Better yet, you are a good looking person (at least that is what your mom tells you) you take them back to the barracks that night or the following week and have sex with them. In 3 months you are getting married (don't forget I'm being nice). You think you are in love and now you have this thought in your mind that he or she loves you. Until problems come, then she is sleeping with another man while you were on deployment, I mean men (plural), spending more money than you make, out partying all the time, getting fat, not working but just staying at home chilling watching TV, eating all the 2011 snacks you got off bootleg. You were her meal ticket to leaving her parents house once you had that "Pillow Talk." If you don't know what pillow talk is, I'm going to explain it. You have sex, not normal sex, but mind-blowing sex. We are all adults so I can be real. Afterwards the two of you are lying in bed on the pillows looking either at the ceiling or at each other. Then you start talking, the lights are off, and the room is quiet because your roommate is out at the club trying to get a yang jank too. Then the pillow releases emotions. You say, "I love you" and she says, "I do too." Then the pillow talk goes on and on, 3 months go by (Hello, me being nice) and now you are going to your leadership and saying, "I'm getting married."

Solution:

Don't get caught up in your feelings or that pillow. First, if you want to have sex with someone (if you decided not to wait for marriage), respect yourself and that someone enough to wait. Ladies, if you want to see how much this guy really likes you tell him you want to wait a minimum of 6 months and see if he stays around and does the same "nice guy" things he did when he first met you. I would say 1 out of every 15-20 guys might. Guys, before you decide to have sex with her (if you don't decide to wait till marriage), do this: Talk to her for a couple of weeks. Stay away from the club where you met her for those weeks, then just pop up and watch how she acts. You are wondering how you will know she is there. Trust me; if you met her there she will be there. See who she dances with and how many times she gives her number out. If she walks in the club and many different men know her from seeing her at the club, and not because she is a well-known real estate agent, she probably gets around. If you happen to be stationed overseas when you go to bars and clubs that are known for Americans being there, the foreign women usually speak pretty good English. Just know that she is probably not there for the good music. My brothers, don't let what is between her legs blind you into thinking she loves you or you are in love. I warn men because they seem to be the victims. Enjoy the company of the opposite sex; that doesn't mean you have to have sex with all of them. Everybody has something with them or what I like to call a "first met you". You were not like this when I first met you. Time will always tell you about a person, just be patient. This might be a shocker to you, but you should try dating. I know all you young people are wondering what that is. I'm going to give you my meaning. Dating is when you spend time outside of the bed to get to know someone.

Problem:

Don't do it! Don't do it! Don't do it! I talked about Lonely Mcknightus in the beginning. Enlist men, he is out there. Most of the divorces in the armed forces happen in the first 4 years of a person's military career. Lonely Mcknightus being around plays a big factor. When I was in the Marines I would say about half of the Marines who were first termers were married. I would say over half of that half are now divorced. I will tell you a some of the reasons why they are divorced. One reason is that they didn't take advantage of being single and they let their feelings of loneliness drive them into marriage. Another reason is because of the terrible barracks living conditions. When you get married you can live in base housing or you can live off base. I think another reason they get divorced is because they realize, "Damn, what the hell did I just do? I was just lonely." They often don't love the person; they just like how they make them feel: NOT ALONE. Over time that and other emotions die down and real life problems come. Better example, when the dust settles you can see clearly.

Solution:

Did you know that you don't have to be in a marriage or relationship to not be lonely? The world (people) says if you are married or in a relationship you are not lonely. Here is the crazy part, you can be in a marriage or relationship and still be lonely. Get a hobby. Think about something that you might like to do and try it. Meet people other than military personnel who enjoy something you enjoy, or find good positive military members to hang with. The key word is "positive." Just because they buy you a round doesn't mean they are good people. You have been warned that Lonely Mcknightus is walking around in those barracks and while you are in boot camp or basic training. Fight him off with fun activities that keep you busy and your mind off loneliness, depression and home sickness. That way you won't have to deal with the headache that comes with being married at a young age. Nine out of ten men wish they were single. Go ask your dad what he would do if your mom was to leave him. The answer might shock you. I'm not going to tell you not to get married. I'm lying; actually, I am. Seriously, trust me on this one. Date her or him for 4 years. I know that is long and if you were a civilian you would date for like 2 to 3 years before getting married. The military is a different ball game. I have a great deal of respect for military wives (who are faithful and committed to their husbands). I say that because you will have deployments, training, field time, mandatory this and that's. She will be alone often. Can she handle that? Can she be supportive when she is lonely? Can she take care of the home when you are not there? Can she be committed to you and not be shaking her ass at the club while you are in the field? There is so much involved being a military wife; not all can do some of those things. Especially at the ages of 18, 19, or 20. Past one enlistment she will be older. To me that means she will be a little more mature, so she can see what your job entails and can understand what she is getting into. I have often heard, "Hey, baby, I'm at my first station, marry me, you just graduated high school 4 months ago. Fellas and ladies trust me on this one.

8. Spend Most Of Their Money On Alcohol

Problem:

Too much of anything can be a bad thing. Alcohol can be viewed in different ways. For those who spend most of their money on alcohol, remember this: Alcohol can be a drug (DRUG - any substance that, when absorbed into the body of a living organism alters normal bodily function) and an addiction. If you are deciding between eating a five-dollar chicken box at KFC because you are hungry or buying fifth of cognac, you have a problem. I have seen this same situation many times when I have walked into the alcohol stores on base with different Marines. I always see the excitement in their eyes and expression when they see the liquor they love. The funny part is that each bottle of alcohol that we pass on the shelf, that they have tried, comes with a story. For example, when you read the names--Grey Goose, Henny, Bacardi Mojito, Jack and coke, Jägerbomb, Patrón—does it strike a nerve? Did you clap, or did you say to yourself, "I got some of that in the fridge?" Then maybe you understand where I'm coming from.

Solution:

Drinking can be fun, but do it in moderation. Don't let most of your income, I'm sorry, all of your income go to alcohol. Expand your leisure activities and spend money on things that are fun and different. Recovering in the morning is not fun to most people, but to some people it might be. When you are recovering you have or are losing time in your life that could have been used doing something constructive or entertaining. I say that because you spend one day or night drinking and the next recovering, and then you are off to work the next day. Some military members drink on the recovery day without regard to the 8-hour rule. All I'm saying is: open your options to different experiences that are fun and give your life enjoyment.

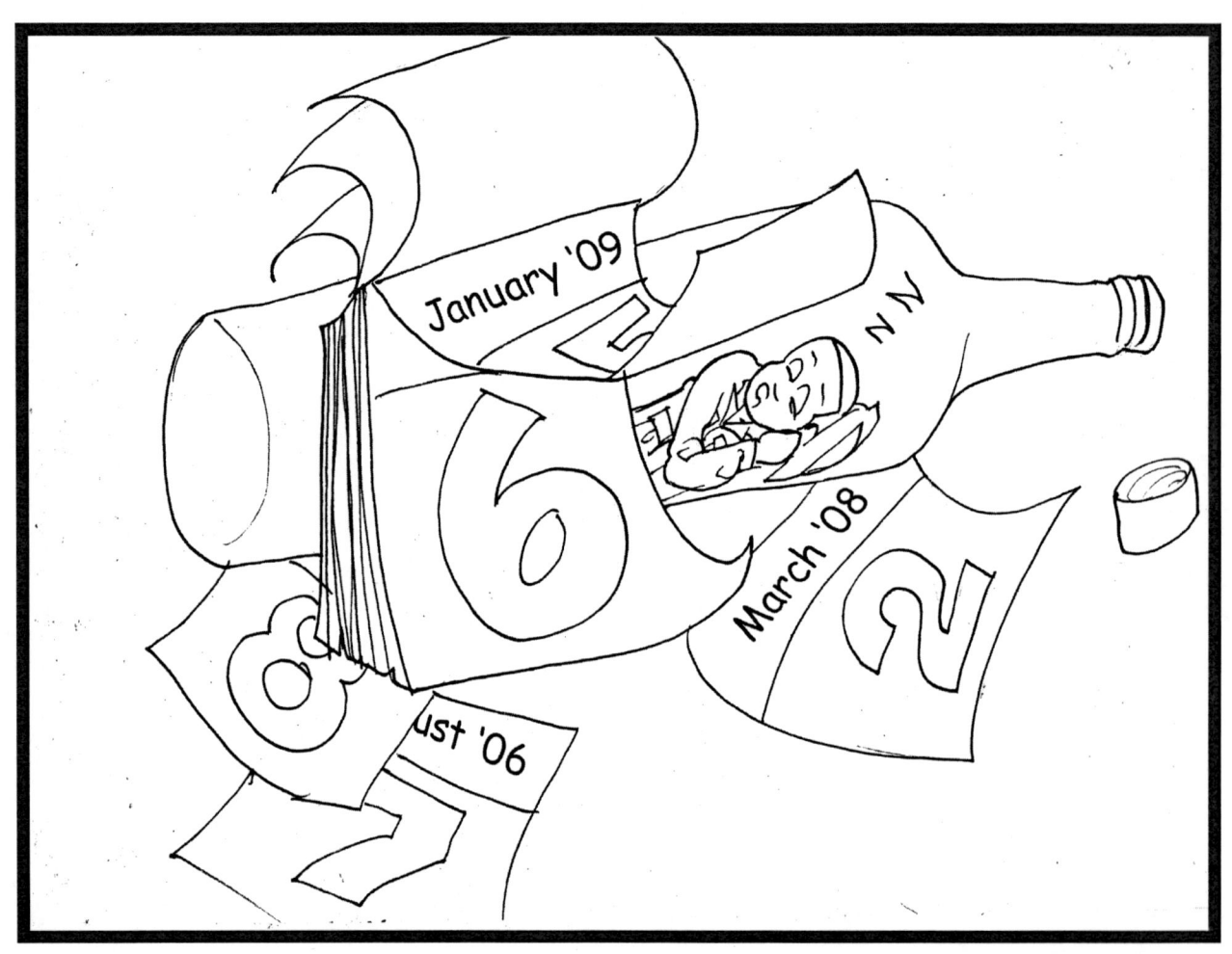

9. Drink Their Enlistment Away

Problem:

I can't tell you, my enlist men, how many military members I have seen drink their enlistment away. Then they look back and wonder where their enlistment went. Don't spend 4 years recovering from the night before. There are 52 weeks in a year, which means there are 52 Sundays in a year. That equals a little over a month and a half (me being nice). This means you have wasted time that could have been used doing something that could better you. I have seen many of my buddies kick themselves in the butt because they did not attend school or travel the area that they were in. They got off work on Friday, went to what Marines call a 7-day store, got their beer or liquor drink and ordered pizza. They look back and are like, "Where did the 4 years go?" It went into recovering and drinking.

Solution:

Did you know that the Military has something called TUITION ASSISTANCE? TA offers financial assistance to service members who elect to pursue Off-Duty or Voluntary Education. TA funds 100% of tuition costs for high school completion up to a fiscal year TA cap of $4,500. That allows you to further your education and put something into you other than alcoholic beverages, which most of you lightweights throw up any way. Unless you are one of the old players who wears jean shorts and black dress shoes with the long white socks that are loose at the top. Those are the experienced drinkers. If you are in a new area fill up the car and go for a drive and travel the area. I remember coming back home and my friends talking about something and I was often saying I have been there, seen it, and done it and I just turned 25. Think about how most people spend their lives saving for a vacation that lasts for 2 or 3 weeks. As an enlist men, you could be living any number of interesting places, like Spain, Germany, Japan, Korea, California, or Texas. Don't drink those opportunities to experience new things away. Don't look back and say 4 years went by and I drank my enlistment away.

Problem:

I like this topic because it is so funny. Recruiters are like car salesmen except the gain is much greater. A car sales man will lie to you to make you sign on the dotted line so that you drive off the lot. Then you can't sit down because the shaft they gave you was so thick. A recruiter will promise and tell you certain things so that you join, just like a car salesman would do to get you to buy a car. They give you the entire positive, which is true, but they don't always give you the reality, (some do and some don't). When you walk into the recruiter's station they are going to smile at you and ask you if you want to join the best… whatever branch that might be. This is true; every branch is different but at the same time every branch is the best at WHAT THEY DO. The Marine Corps is the first to fight; every Marine is a rifleman. The grunts 0311 don't like that saying because they are rifleman and they don't believe every Marine does what they do. Marines go in and do damage. If you are thinking that you are not going to deploy, you are wrong. Over 50 percent of Marines deploy at 8-12 months at a time. There are a lot more soldiers than Marines and their deployments can be longer. I do like the enlistment bonus they give. The Air Force is like being a civilian in uniform, and I've heard this straight from the horse's mouth. They have plenty of money, so they are the ones with the new stuff and the nice things. The Navy drops off the Marines and patches them up. Their deployments can range from 6 months to a year, not on land but on the sea… in boats. I know you have seen the Navy commercials. Planes taking off, special ops fast roping off the helicopter with M16's, a high tech boat doing corvette z06 speeds, then the music playing and all of the shipmates are standing on the edge of the ship. Then you are thinking to yourself, "I want to do that," and that is what the recruiter is going to play. In your mind you are thinking that is what it is like. Then you go home and tell your entire family, "I'm going to be diving off boats, shooting the enemy, leaning off the side of mini boats with guns, and playing basketball on the ship while laughing and having a great time." Just like that sexy girl you saw in the club who was sexy till she had a big ass key and keyed the hell out of your car. She looked good till she gave you that "first met you". The picture recruiters paint is perfect, but there is a lot of reality that is not told.

Solution:

I don't want you to think all recruiters are like the car sales men because they are not. Their job is to get people to join the armed forces. In order to do that they sometimes may tell you certain things that not completely true or don't paint the whole picture. Then you look back and say, "Wow! My recruiter lied or didn't tell me this." No, he or she did'nt and you now are obligated to a 4-year contract. Let me tell you something. In those 4 years of your first enlistment you will reach a level of discipline, experience, and knowledge that will set you apart from your peers who didn't join. The discipline, experience, and knowledge that you will take from the military will be life changing. That is if you join with the intentions to make yourself better, and that's something that you couldn't replace. I say go and find people who have been in for 4 to 8 years. Ask them the truth about the branch you want to join. Know that everybody's experiences are going to be different but life changing. Don't go to someone who got kicked out for selling or smoking drugs. A lot of them think the military was wrong for kicking them out. Ask successful enlisted members or officers what they think. Ask them about the jobs that they do, and their, experiences, and then formulate your own opinion. They were probably lied to also, and they might go with you to the recruiting station so they can read through the BS and tell you if they are lying. If you don't get the ASVAB score you want, who cares? The Tuition Assistance and the GI bill can allow you to further your education once you join. This will really set you apart from your peers. Plus you can retake the test 30 days later. Know what you are getting into, because 4 active and 4 years inactive (I.R.R program) is what you will be signing up for. When you get in, do what is right and enjoy yourself. There are so many cultures and new things to see and do. After you look back at those 4 years you would never want to replace them. The experience is life changing.

11. Think They Have An Opinion

Problem:

I thought I was "Mr. Smart E. Man" when I first joined. I really thought if I made a suggestion or expressed an opinion it was going to be heard. Wrong! I was the boot, new booty, the FNG ("freaking new guy" rated PG). I just needed to clean and do what I was told. Many people think like I did when they first join. They think they are joining an organization in which their opinion counts. That is not how it works, enlist men. You will find yourself getting yelled at or getting played with (you will understand when you join). So, for the first couple of years you don't have an opinion. Unless you are $#!% hot and there is even a fine line for that. When I made it to my first station after school, I had duty on Christmas, then the Fourth of July. Plus I had to clean all the time. These are things that you can expect when being the new guy.

Solution:

The chain of command is how the military works. The heavier your collar is the more your voice can be heard and mean something. When you first join, your collar still gets blown over by the wind outside because there is no rank to hold it down. The first couple of years are going to suck. I repeat things throughout this book for a reason. So I'll say it again. Your first couples of years are going to suck. That is because you are not in a leadership position; you are in a troop. I would like for you to sit back--not literally--but sit back, go to work, and observe and learn everything that is going on around you. Learn from it and use it when your time comes. Meaning when your collar starts getting heavy, then you can make different changes or express a personal opinion. You will be able to voice an opinion and make choices because you are the head person in charge. When you say "jump", everybody is going to say, "Sir or Mama, how high?" The definition of leadership or to lead is: The ability to influence someone to follow one's decision. I say that because once you get to that point don't be telling people to jump. Don't forget where you came from, don't burn bridges and know that once you are in a position of power you should use it to help a group of Soldiers, Marines, Shipmates, Airmen or Coast guardians. The same people you are telling to jump might be the same ones you are going to need in combat. Think about this, if you spend 20 years in the military, only 3-4 are spent as a troop. The remainder is in a leadership position.

12. Marry A Woman Who Knows More About The Military Then Them

Problem:

Beware, my enlist men brothers! I say "brothers" because they are the ones that seem to be the victims. When I was stationed in California I loved it, but there is something funny about California. Certain places were known to have Marines there. For example, any marine that was stationed California there knows this place called "Devil Dog Mall." It is located in Oceanside, California. Oceanside is known for the ocean and the Marines. The women down there know that you are a Marine by your haircut and your dorky boot camp graduation ceremony walk. They know when you get paid, how much you get paid, the medical you get, the nice on base housing you get if you're married, and the list goes on and on. You could actually learn something from them. This doesn't just apply to Marines in Oceanside; this applies to all branches at all major bases. They know where you are going to hang out and they know how to rub their bunson on you and smile to get your attention. They will tell you whatever is necessary to get your attention. Think about it you are 18, 19, or 20 and back home no woman has told you that you are sexy. You don't turn into a GQ magazine man of the year once you join the military. The only thing sexy about you is your benefits. You still wear your tight ass jeans to your nipples. So tight I could count the amount of change in your pants from the bar. That is not sexy, you are not sexy, and she wants a way out of her life at home with her mom and dad. So you have sex with her and you think you did a good job because you have been taking Extends pills and reading Playboy magazines. She tells you, you are the best she ever had and she wants to be with you… WRONG! What she means is you have the best benefits and she wants your money.

Solution:

First stop taking Extends. Anything with a side effect of an erection lasting 4 hours or longer is not healthy. Ladies, I know it sounds fun, but when he is at work and he is erect from 8 to noon, is not good thing. Second, if she is educating you on your benefits and she wants to marry you, she is probably looking for a way out of her parents' house. Don't marry her! Have a good time and enjoy her company; that doesn't mean you have to have sex with her and marry her. I know the feeling of companionship is a good feeling, but take your time and enjoy being single with no kids or single with kids. Buy a large pizza, eat one slice and throw the rest away; you can do that when you are single. When you eat, your whole family eats. If she gets on your nerves, (and she will) delete her number and move on to the next friend. But don't marry her! Take your time; make sure that you have no doubts. Also make sure you are financially and mentally stable enough to make that lifelong covenant with that man or woman. If you have more questions talk to your Chaplain.

13. Go A.W.O.L. or U.A.

Problem:

I want you to know, enlist men, that 9 times out of 10 you are going to deploy, meaning you're going to be sent somewhere to the fight. So, if you believed the recruiters when he said you might not go because for one reason or another, you were wrong for believing them. It might come as a shock, but if you decide to run from Uncle Sam he is going to find you, lock you up, and then kick you out with a an Other Than Honorable (OTH), Bad Conduct(Bad Chicken Dinner)or a Dishonorable (which is the equivalent of a felony conviction, only worse) discharge. Once you go to jail and have some involuntary man to man jail sex because you didn't keep your head up and your ass down, Uncle Sam is going to give you the boot. And ladies, you are not exempt from woman to woman jail sex either; it happens. Keep in mind that companies that hold government contracts often require their employees to be eligible for various degrees of security clearance. You may or may not be qualified to receive a clearance level due to an Other than Honorable discharge. Yes, people, that means McDonalds. If you get a bad chicken dinner virtually all veterans' benefits are forfeited by a Bad Conduct Discharge. If you get a dishonorable discharge you can try and get a job cutting grass, and I don't feel sorry for you. You can recover from these things in time but why put yourself through the headache and pain? You are going to deploy. I repeat YOU ARE GOING TO DEPLOY!

Solution:

You signed on the dotted line, so it doesn't matter if you feel like you got the shaft without dinner and a condom. You still signed on that dotted line and you should have educated and prepared yourself on what to expect going into the Armed Forces. Do you think you are the only one who has a wife who is going to be giving birth to your first child while you are on deployment? WRONG! Many have come before you and many will come after you. They have given up family time and their families to do what they signed on the dotted line to do. Sorry, enlist men. Stop feeling sorry for yourself and thinking nobody has it worse than you, and go get some because if we don't do it, who will?

14. Follow The Wrong Crowds

Problem:

Yes there are wrong crowds in the military just like in the streets, schools and workplace. You will see military members who don't adjust. They go to work late and get article 15's all the time. (If you don't know what article 15 is, "Wiki it"). They don't try and get their $#!% (not rated PG) together even though they have been in for 6 years and they are still E-3's. Those are not the military members that you should be hanging out with. People can have 2 kinds of influence on you good or bad. Better yet, show me the company you keep and I can tell you who you are. That's what big mama used to say. I don't have one but I saw it on TV However you will find yourself going in the same direction as they did career-wise and maybe worse.

Solution:

Watch the company you keep. If you are going to have a circle put positive people in it, people who are steadily trying to be better in all aspects of their life. Be the one who sets the positive example to follow. When people view you in a positive light and they have nothing but good things to say, you will find yourself going a lot further in your career.

15. Go Home And Lie

Problem:

Come on, enlist men, stop feeding your friends those lies when you go on leave! If you are a cook, tell them you are a cook. Many military members go home and tell their family and friends that when they were overseas they killed 20 insurgents and saved 5 lives. But in actuality they deep fried 20 chickens and served it with 5 different sides. Some go to extremes and put ribbons and medals on their uniforms that they didn't earn. Some get caught, and you can get in trouble for wearing a silver star (that is your 3rd award) that you haven't earned.

Solution:

Fry your chickens and make your biscuits and be proud. Make the bomb digity sides for the military members serving over there like you are. Be the one person people come to because you put your all into whatever you do. Same team, different type of fight. You are an important factor in whatever job you do, so enjoy it and give it your all. If you want to be on the front lines getting some like the movie 300, try and change your job. If that doesn't work join the Marines and ask for 0311, or join the Army and ask for infantry; they will hook you up. Be honest to yourself, friends and family.

16. Do Drugs

Problem:

Enlist men, really! Is that how you feel? I want you to think about what and why you have decided to join the Armed Forces. I know you didn't join to smoke some weed or sniff cocaine. You could have done that on the street. You joined for a change. Take the old you and leave it on the street, the block, or the trailer park. I know drug dealers try to get you with their simple pitches. It's funny how they say everything twice fast. "Got that kush got that kush, got that fire got that fire, got that purp got that purp". You don't get it? Say it fast two times stay away! Don't let their simple marketing pitches get you.

Solution:

I have a perfect solution. Don't start doing drugs so you won't have to worry about quitting. It is not 'if' you get caught, it's 'when' you get caught. Then you are standing tall in front of your Company Commander saying that you are sorry that you did it. In reality you are sorry you got caught because you knew what you were doing. So when they bust you down, meaning take your rank and kick you out, don't be surprised. Most people go home and tell their parents that they were hurt and got separated, right before they killed 20 insurgents and saved 5 Soldiers lives. So just say "No" and leave the old smoking weed, crack sniffing you behind and start a new more fulfilling life. Remember: Wherever your mind goes your heart goes, and then your actions follow.

17. Get Contract Marriages

Problem:

This not only happens with enlist men, but also in all service member years, but that is not the name of this book. I know that you are wondering what a contract marriage is, so check the "STUPID THINGS DICTIONARY" in the back. When it comes to contract marriages it can be dangerous and costly. It can seem to be financially beneficial to untrained enlist men. This is how it happens. You get your pay check and you think it is too small because you are not looking at the big picture. So you say to yourself, "I can't afford this brand new car I just bought because I bought it before I bought Donte's book, "Stupid Things People do when they first join the Military." Then you say to yourself, "I need a contract marriage so that I can get more money, move out of the nasty barracks and not have a roommate who smells like a full court press." There are two kinds of contract marriages, but both are meant to gain more money. One is with someone you know who is willing to help you out for a piece of the pie and the other is for a green card. I had a person offer me $10,000 for a green card (meaning a woman). Of course I took it, yeah right, let's be for real! For those of you who meet a woman or man who is not an American citizen, and you decide to marry them so they can have a green card, you are looking at 5 years not dropping the soap, and a healthy $250,000 fine. You could have gone to college, had your degree paid for by Uncle Sam, then submitted an Officer package and become an Officer of whatever branch of service, and made what you would have made with a contract marriage without looking at possible jail time and a bad chicken dinner (Bad Conduct Discharge). The funny thing to me is when a military member actually does it and they can't find their wife, then reality kicks in.

Solution:

This is not a hard solution. Why risk your career or shorten your enlistment for a couple hundred or a thousand bucks a paycheck? I was in the same money situation before and I thought about a contract marriage. I think that we have all thought about it at some point in time. For me, I didn't do it because I believe marriage is something that shouldn't be played around with for money. I think that when a man finds a wife he finds a good thing. It is something that is special and should be done because of love and commitment. Not to live out in town or for personal gain. So, think about your morals and if that doesn't work, think about involuntary jail sex.

Problem:

This subject applies to everybody, but mostly first termers. There is nothing wrong with having a drink. You have to be responsible when doing so. You will get safety briefs just about every Friday before you secure for weekend liberty (which is not a right, but a privilege). Yes, that is correct. Liberty is not a right but a privilege. You will see no matter how many briefs you get, somebody will always turn up after the weekend or a 96 with a DUI. They lose rank and get "45 and 45." If you don't know what 45 and 45 is, "Wiki it". So that E-4 that you worked hard to get is now an E-3, depending on whether or not you were even of age to drink. If you are under 21 and you get a DUI that E-4 is now an E-2.

Solution:

Don't do it. There are many cab companies that will drop you off on base, and I'm sure your command (if it is a good command) will have a pot of money that is used for military members (just like yourself) who may be too drunk to drive. You call a cab and the command pays for it. Then you simply pay it back so the next enlistee can use it. When you drink and drive you endanger the lives of others and yourself. I really can't make this topic funny, and if you get caught I hope they take your rank.

19. Don't Use Contraceptives

Problem:

This happens all the time. You go out, meet a man or woman, get naked and don't use protection. I don't mean a flack and Kevlar. I'm talking about condoms. I know you don't want the "CLAP", the "DRIP" or the "BURN". There are diseases out there that can't be cured, meaning you will have them for life. I had a friend that didn't use a condom and got bad credit. That might not be forever but it takes years to clear up. Seriously, I know you see a fine young man or woman and you wonder how they feel. We are adults, be real, but that real feeling you want can turn into bumps and brown pee. Tell him or her, "You are sexy, but you are not worth my life."

Solution:

Simple. If you are still broke from the high car payments, go to the on base hospital and they will give you some condoms. They are free and small. If not, spend some of your liquor money and buy some. For those who get sex by luck only or because the girl notices you have on Swagger from Old Spice, get one from the barracks guy or girl who is always bringing a different women or men to their room every weekend. I'm sure they have contraceptives they can lend you. When you get a chance stop in at medical, flip open one of the herpes handouts; yes, that is what it looks like. Guys, it looks like a Johnsonville bratwurst that has been on the grill too long. For others struggling in that department, it looks like mini links that have been on the grill too long. Ladies, for you it looks like old roast beef with mold and probably smells like hot dog water. Why experience this? WEAR PROTECTION!

20. Don't Save Money

Problem:

This is a very common mistake that we are all guilty of: not giving back to ourselves. We get paid on the 1st and 15th. Most of the time enlist men are broke on the 1st and on the 15th, others on the 30th and 14th. I remember being so glad there was a galley and free room and board. If not I would have been skinny and living on the street. I know that you want to be fresh and buy all the things that your parents wouldn't let you, like 3 pair of shoes at one time, Coach purses, or an 80 dollar pair of jeans. I want to tell you something you might not know. Those jeans are made of cotton, the same material that Wal-Mart's jeans are made of. They just don't say Bathing-Apes or Ed Hardy. A woman has never said to me, "I wasn't going to give you my number, but since you have an Ed Hardy shirt on you can have it." Have you ever taken a woman on a date and been so broke that, you ordered water? Then when it was time to order food you said, "I'm really not that hungry. I ate earlier." Ladies, you have it easy. However, if he goes to the bathroom or makes a phone call every time right before the check comes, and if this happens then you might want to find a different guy. Not only is he broke but he also might have cheap man syndrome.

Solution:

When I learned about money management through making financial mistakes that ended with being broke all the time, I started to pay myself. I would take %10 to pay tithe, and take another 10% to put away in savings (and sometimes more). If a female wanted to go on a date, dollar menu at McDonalds. If I wanted to impress her, I would tell her she could get the Quarter Pounder WITH cheese. If she can eat with me at McDonalds then she can eat with me at a 5-star restaurant. It is ok to be cheap, AKA frugal. Watch and manage your money, and pay yourself first. Invest in YOU so that when YOU need it YOU have it. Never give anybody your last dollar; being broke is not a good feeling. Think about the big picture not the small picture. Must I say it again? READ! There are dozens of informative books out there to help you, so educate yourself.

Problem:

I wonder what enlist men are thinking sometimes. I don't think that they are thinking straight. This is what I have seen happen whether guy or girl; I use guys mostly because those seem to be the victims. Once again your girlfriend or boyfriend didn't raise you. Your mom, dad, or grand-ma has put up with you for 18 or 19 years of your life thus-far. They have spent money, time, and energy into giving you a good life. You know that you gave your parents hell through your teenage years. You know what I mean, trying to keep up with the fads, asking for money, sneaking out of the house, thinking your parents don't understand you. That is another book in itself. I can go on all day about teenagers. However, your parents have been taking care of you and dealing with your BS for years. The boyfriend or girlfriend you are with did not raise you. The only thing they have given you is feelings, emotions, hugs, kisses, and sometimes some chittee chittee. Do you think you should sign over a $400,000 life insurance policy to someone who you have only known for a little while? My dad told me this and I believe it is true: He said, "Son, nobody in this world loves you and cares for you like me and your mother do." I want you to think about that statement, but think about your parents saying it to you. What feeling do you get? Think about the person you are with and how many times they have broken up with you because you were being a "jive turkey". It was you calling them to tell him or her that you wanted them back. Do you really think they care as much as your mom and dad?

Solution:

Simple. When you join and the admin section asks you whose name you want on your life insurance policy as beneficiaries, make sure you say the names of the ones who raised you. If your girlfriend or boyfriend gets mad, leave them. You can see where their heart is. My favorite phrase is, "We are getting married one day, and don't you want it to go to me?" Yeah right, I met you on Myspace!

Stupid Things Dictionary:

Google it - searching Google to obtain information regarding a subject.

Enlist men - A person who is about to join or has recently joined the United States armed forces.

First met you - a phase that refers to the things you didn't see in a person when you first met them.

FNG - the freaking new guy (rated PG -13 version).

$#!% Hot - refers to a person that is really good at all levels of their military career.

Liberty – see "Wiki it."

Article 15 - see "Wiki it."

Restriction – see "Wiki it."

Smoke pit – a place where military member and sometimes barracks girls go to smoke.

Barracks Girls - (Rated PG-13 version) -women who are in the military and some that are not who engages in sexual intercourse with many male service members sometimes all at once.

Cheap man syndrome – A sickness that strikes you when you realize you have little to no money until pay-day.

Leave – paid vacation for the military 2.5 days a month for active duty.

Non Commissioned Officer – see "Wiki it."

Yang Jank - a woman from the ages of 18-22 or 5–10 years younger than you.

Bunson – large or normal size booty.

Wiki it - Wikipedia

Author's Notes:

I want to thank you for purchasing and reading my book. My name is Donte' Sams, and I was in the United States Marine Corps for 4 years. I have been to 3 different stations: Camp Pendleton, CA, Rota, Spain, and Norfolk, VA. When I was at those stations I saw the crazy and stupid things military members do in all branches. It all seems to be the same because of the age group that joins. It is not my intention to call anybody stupid or offend anybody. It's just truthful humor because nobody is stupid; we all sometimes make bad decisions. The bad decision- making can turn into good decision-making through time, and trial and error. I know if it weren't for God's grace I wouldn't have earned my honorable discharge. I say that because I have made many STUPID decisions and there are more to come. There is nobody in this world that is going to get it right the first time. I didn't; I'm not perfect and neither are you. Learning from your mistakes and learning from others is the key. When I wrote this book I took serious topics and kept them serious, but put some humor in it through art-work and words. Whatever mistakes you have made, learn from them and give that knowledge to someone to help make them successful, no matter what branch they are in or have served in. We are defending our flag, country, and the American constitution. We help keep the flag standing. Pass this book to another military member. Maybe something that you told them is in this book and they can see you weren't saying it just to be saying it. Enjoy your time and push hard for success. If you make a bad decision, get up, brush it off and keep push forward because you can't change the past. If you decide to get out after the first 4 or 8 years, get out with something, education and experience, whatever it is that is going to make you better. Know that God has a purpose for you in your life, and He loves you more than I can explain or imagine. There are two kinds of people: dreamers and chasers. Everybody dreams but not everybody chases. So be a chaser and chase your dreams.